THE
PRE-NATAL
ASSIGNMENT

THE
PRE-NATAL
ASSIGNMENT

A Journey Into Your Prophetic Destiny

Before I formed thee in the belly I knew thee; and before thou camest forth out of the womb I sanctified thee, and I ordained thee a prophet unto the nations. Jeremiah 1:5 (KJV)

Dr. Angela M. Rucker

authorHOUSE®

AuthorHouse™
1663 Liberty Drive
Bloomington, IN 47403
www.authorhouse.com
Phone: 1-800-839-8640

Take note that the name satan and related names are not capitalized. We choose not to acknowledge him, even to the point of violating grammatical rules.

Published by AuthorHouse   10/19/2012

ISBN: 978-1-4772-7816-1 (sc)
ISBN: 978-1-4772-7817-8 (e)

Library of Congress Control Number: 2012918749

This book is printed on acid-free paper.

The Pre-Natal Assignment
A Journey Into Your Prophetic Destiny

Jeremiah 1:4–10 (KJV)

4 Then the word of the LORD came unto me, saying,

5 Before I formed thee in the belly I knew thee; and before thou camest forth out of the womb I sanctified thee, and I ordained thee a prophet unto the nations.

6 Then said I, Ah, Lord GOD! behold, I cannot speak: for I am a child.

7 But the LORD said unto me, Say not, I am a child: for thou shalt go to all that I shall send thee, and whatsoever I command thee thou shalt speak.

8 Be not afraid of their faces: for I am with thee to deliver thee, saith the LORD.

9 Then the LORD put forth his hand, and touched my mouth. And the LORD said unto me, Behold, I have put my words in thy mouth.

10 See, I have this day set thee over the nations and over the kingdoms, to root out, and to pull down, and to destroy, and to throw down, to build, and to plant.

Preface

For years, I lived a life lacking revelation of who I really was and what was required of me. Because I had no convictions of my own, I was forced to accept whatever was presented to me. I allowed people to package me however they saw fit. My definition of self was consistent with their definition of me. I was in bondage to people's opinion of me and enslaved to the lies they would tell me.

My quest for self-discovery haunted me for many years. Now that I have discovered the truth that governs the questions that I had, I am motivated to share my findings in this book. The pages provide meaningful answers to hard questions and offer life-changing truths.

The questions of my youth lingered for years and accompanied me to a place where self-discovery challenged me to free myself from mental slavery. I was familiar with who I was, but it was not until I understood the essence of who I was, before I was born, that I got to know the real me. We will never find the truth about our existence until we discover the truth about our pre-natal assignment.

We will never find the truth about our existence until we discover the truth about our pre-natal assignment.

In an effort to cope, many have settled for the easy and mundane course that keeps them in a place of comfort, which requires very little of them and keeps them bound in mediocrity. The abundant life demands faith to seek and discover, courage to ascend into heights of unknown regions, and determination to seek after truth that liberates and releases self from any form of bondage.

The key to living the abundant life is to obtain knowledge, understanding, and wisdom. We need knowledge that is designed to teach us who we are from God's perspective. Without this form of knowledge, we become like a reed in a desert land without any source of nourishment that is conducive to growth and development. The Bible says, "My people perish for a lack of knowledge." (Hosea 4:6)

We need understanding so that we can tap into purpose. Knowledge provides "the what" and understanding gives us "the why." Wisdom reveals "the how" and it teaches us how to apply what we know.

Proverbs 4:5-8 (KJV)
5 Get wisdom, get understanding: forget it not; neither decline from the words of my mouth.

6 Forsake her not, and she shall preserve thee: love her, and she shall keep thee.

7 Wisdom is the principal thing; therefore get wisdom: and with all thy getting get understanding.

8 Exalt her, and she shall promote thee: she shall bring thee to honor, when thou dost embrace her.

As you turn the pages of this book, my hope is that you will be inspired to embark upon your own journey of self-discovery. My prayer is that you will be liberated from every form of ignorance that would attempt to enslave you and cause you to be a stranger to your prophetic destiny.

Be free and stay free!

Foreword

Self-discovery is the means by which we are able to dig deep into our lives to obtain significance and purpose. No person can reach the zenith of their destiny unless they embark upon a journey that reveals the truth about their genesis. Every ship out in the ocean needs a compass to direct the course of their voyage. Self-discovery serves as the compass that directs the course of life.

You cannot embrace purpose and walk into your destiny without discovering self. Self- discovery takes you beyond your present station to a time before birth when you were first conceived in the mind of God. The beginning of self is before self. Therefore, self can only be discovered if you are willing to go beyond the boundaries of self-reasoning and enter into a realm that challenges you to believe the incomprehensible.

Dr. Angela Rucker addresses very serious questions that speak to the reason for your existence and the very source of your life. She challenges you to embark upon your own personal journey of self-discovery and to recognize that, before you were formed in the womb, you were selected by God and given a particular assignment to carry out in the earth.

The Pre-Natal Assignment exposes real life challenges on the journey to your destiny. It inspires you to dig deeper and to reach higher until you arrive at a place where you discover the truth about who you are, whose you are, and why you were born.

The door to greatness is open to everyone who will carry out their pre-natal assignment. The principles that are intertwined between the pages of this book will allow you to enter into that place of greatness.

I recommend this book to all those who desire to discover the real significance of life.

Rev. Dr. Geraldine Miggins

Introduction

As a little girl, I always wondered why I was born and how many angels brought me here. I had this weird idea that I was escorted from another place, by angels, and was dropped off on earth and presented to my parents. I would sit under the almond tree, in Jamaica, while I braided grass—pretending that the patches of grass, with their long blades, were my children.

I would have very long and interrogating conversations with Ann, or Sue, or Ginger, whichever one I felt like talking to that day. I would talk to them about my theory that I was brought to earth for a reason and one day I would discover the reason. My theory was even more far-fetched because it supported the notion that after I had carried out the purpose for which I was dispatched, I would be picked up by the same angels who dropped me off and they would carry me back to the place of my genesis. It is amazing how close I was to the truth and did not know it. The part about being dropped off was a little stretched, but I found out later on in life that I was on the right track, for I was indeed dispatched from eternity with a purpose.

It took many years of searching to find the real me, and endless questions about my real identity, to arrive at a place of truth and understanding that led to self-discovery.

It wasn't until I understood that God is a God of purpose and I was born with a purpose that I was able to discover the "me" who I was created to be.

Once I realized that my purpose for being dispatched to my mother's womb was more than just biology, but to carry out a divine assignment, I purposed in my heart to glorify God by fulfilling my assignment. I was determined to make a difference. Since then, my search for purpose has been unrelentless and deliberate and my appointment with my prophetic destiny has been all-consuming.

Many people accept a life of mundane eventualities with an attitude of indifference. Others accept mediocrity as God's best for their lives. Then there are those who can't even bother to figure out their present circumstance—*Que Sera, Sera.* None of the above choices are conducive to germinating the seed of greatness that lies within.

Diligence and determination, coupled with the understanding of my divine assignment, are the thrust and velocity of my life. The road to self-discovery is a journey that leads you to your purpose. The path might be circuitous and seemingly never ending, but the journey is a source of enlightenment that leads to your destiny.

My world as a child did not allow for questions which engendered real hard answers based on life-changing truths. As a matter of fact, the old adage that children should be seen and not heard was a standard in my house. Whatever questions you had that presented any inclination of a threat to the status quo would be rebuked and you would be silenced one way or another. Ha! That's real old school. You would have a very important question which, if answered, would bring some clarity and perspective, but if it could rock the family boat in any way, you were forbidden to ask. As a result, you were forced to live in ignorance which ultimately condemned you to a life of failure and defeat.

Being the persistent person that I am, I determined that I would find a way to get my questions answered. I figured out that truth is something that should be sought after. Ignorance is a personal choice that leads to bondage. Therefore, I chose to seek after truth which emancipates and liberates.

Ignorance is a personal choice that leads to bondage.

Contents

Chapter One

WHY WAS I BORN?

Life is a gift from God and it is the greatest privilege ever bestowed on any human being. When you take a moment to consider this phenomenon called life, you are summoned to an awareness that causes you to realize how very special you are to be included in the mix. The revelation that you could have been a stone or some inanimate being evokes an appreciation of this wonderful privilege that God has given you. You are not a stone. You are not a piece of wood. You are not undefined matter that occupies space without purpose. You are a human being with the capacity to think, make choices, contribute to humanity, and make a great difference in the earth. Wow! What a privilege!

Just think, after all God had created, creation was not complete without you. Man—the species—was the crowning glory of all of creation. Even after God had made the beautiful expanse, all the stars and planets were in place, vegetation was in place; and even after He had commanded the oceans of the earth to be in existence and not to go beyond their course, God was still not satisfied. His desire to create a full expression of Himself was not complete without man. So, on the sixth day of creation, before He would rest from this divine project, God took the time to fashion man and mold him into His image and after His likeness and then made the awesome declaration, "It is good!"

This means that there is nothing in you that is bad. You can make wrong choices but you are still good. You can mess up and do some of the most ridiculous things but you are still the apex of God's creation. God never makes junk. You are not a mistake. You are His handiwork and a great testimony to the completion of God's creation project. You are here because it was necessary for you to be here. God's plan for the universe would not be complete without you. That's why you are not a stone or a piece of wood. You are God's masterpiece—a living, breathing human being. The amazing thing is that before you were presented to the planet Earth, God knew you.

Psalm 139:14-16 (KJV)
14 I will praise thee; for I am fearfully and wonderfully made: marvellous are thy works; and that my soul knoweth right well.

15 My substance was not hid from thee, when I was made in secret, and curiously wrought in the lowest parts of the earth.

16 Thine eyes did see my substance, yet being unperfect; and in thy book all my members were written, which in continuance were fashioned, when as yet there was none of them.

The textbooks will present to you a scientific scenario of how you came into existence. They will tell you that conception of life for every human being begins as a single cell—formed when father's sperm fertilizes mother's egg.

However, that presentation is based on partial truth and it leaves you with very little understanding of why and how you were placed on the planet Earth. It certainly didn't help me with my "angel theory."

I will submit to you that the real truth about your introduction to life on planet Earth has a greater meaning and is more the result of divine intervention than biology. The creator of planet Earth, Elohim, engineered and devised your whole plan of existence. The reason why you were born is found in Him and He has the creation manual for your life.

Psalm 139:16 (KJV)
16 Thine eyes did see my substance, yet being unperfect; and in thy book all my members were written, which in continuance were fashioned, when as yet there was none of them.

Every fiber of your being has been systematically designed and knitted to accommodate His purpose for your life. God has the master plan for your life and you are special to Him. Just like you would secure your finest china, you are secured by the hand of God. His love secures you and you are guided by His omnipotence, His omniscience, and His omnipresence. By the time you got to Earth you had already been pre-fashioned by God to accommodate a specific purpose and to carry out a divine assignment on this planet.

The following verse of scripture will provide a pre-natal summary of your life:

Jeremiah 1:5 (KJV)
5 Before I formed thee in the belly I knew thee; and before thou camest forth out of the womb I sanctified thee, and I ordained thee a prophet unto the nations.

What does this tell you? The Word of God provides you with a clear understanding that before you were introduced to earth—before the birth experience—the Creator of the universe knew you and He had a relationship with you. Not only did He know you but He formed you. Even in your pre-natal state, God's inescapable presence was with you.

That means even before you were born, God had His hand on you and He designed you according to His vision for your life. Your DNA was coded to accommodate the particular assignment from God for His purpose. Your future was destined before you were born.

Your future was destined before you were born.

So many of us ponder this question: *"WHY WAS I BORN?"* The question of existence visits every generation. Even in the Bible, you see where the prophet who was tagged with the pre-natal assignment asked this very question. This is a question that haunts many of us in moments of diverse challenges.

Jeremiah 20:17-18 (AMP)
17 Because he did not slay me in the womb, so that my mother might have been my grave, and her womb always great.

18 Why did I come out of the womb to see labor and sorrow, that my days should be consumed in shame?

Other haunting questions might be: Am I a mistake? Was I born to suffer and experience pain? What is the reason for my existence? Many answers have been given to these age-old questions. Some have been philosophical, others have been scientific renderings of human reproduction, and some have just been ascribed to metaphysical probings. Solomon, the great prophet of

God, left us with the finest of all answers. His rendering is that God made everything for His own purpose. God is the great manufacturer of your life.

Proverbs 16:4 (KJV)

4 The LORD hath made all things for himself.

Can I just tell you that your life is not a mistake? Even at the worst times and when it seems as though you are facing a dead end, rest in the knowledge that you have an inalienable right to be here on this planet. God sanctioned your life before you were born. You were validated by God in the bosom of eternity.

You were validated by God in the bosom of eternity.

No accolades that man can bestow upon you will ever be greater than the validation that you received from God in your pre-natal state. By the time you were born, you were already authorized and certified to be the greatest person here on earth.

Wow, just the thought of that is incomprehensible. To think that God foreknew me before I was born and took the time to establish my purpose and give me a pre-natal assignment is absolutely mind-blowing. To think that everything about me was fashioned by Him and that He stamped me with a seal of authenticity is so humbling. To know that I am not a stranger to God, but that He knew me before I was conceived in my mother's womb, captures the very core of my being and ignites worship in my soul. God spent time with me before I was born. He knows all about me.

That is so revealing and should liberate so many of you who have been made to think that you have no value or worth. Well, here is a revelation for you. God is infallible and all-knowing. He does not practice trial and error. He is purposeful and everything that He creates is authentic, peculiar, and good. His omniscience covers your beginning and your end. He set the course for your life before you were born. So, your introduction to earth is not scientific. It is one hundred percent divine. The scientific process was designed to facilitate the divine Will of God.

Here is another revelation! Your pre-natal assignment from God is necessary for this planet.

You are here because God has a specific assignment on earth for you to carry out. God singled you out from all the rest to complete a special assignment for His Kingdom. Every cell in your body and your DNA was coded with a specific measure to accomplish this assignment. God did not design you to mal-function. You were designed for success.

Your assignment is for you only and there can be no substitute. Your part to play in God's plan for humanity is reserved strictly for you. There are some who might be able to do a similar job, but there is none who can do it like you. There will always be counterfeits and even the satanic powers of darkness will try to usurp your role, but nothing or anyone can do what God has called you to do. You are it!

It is the heart of God that whatever pre-natal assignment you have been given will be accomplished here on earth for His glory. You will be able to declare as the great Apostle Paul did:

2 Timothy 4:7 (AMP)

7 I have fought the good (worthy, honorable, and noble) fight, I have finished the race, I have kept (firmly held) the faith.

God is counting on you to finish your pre-natal assignment. So, for those of you who, time and time again, have pondered the question "Why was I born?" the best conclusion that I arrived at, as an answer to my own question is, you were born by God for God Himself. You were born to accommodate God's purpose. You were born to carry out a pre-natal assignment.

Knowing that you were born for God's purpose is a fundamental truth that must be entrenched in your heart in order for you to function according to God's plan for your life and to live a life without defeat. Knowledge such as this should propel you into your prophetic destiny and cause you to live a fruitful and productive life. Until you understand that the reason why you were born was not due to some alignment of the stars, but that it was a divine plan of God for you to be a part of humanity, you will continually suffer at the hand of emptiness and insecurity.

Significance is when you know and understand the reason why you are here on planet Earth. You must know that you came here with purpose and by purpose with a pre-natal assignment. You must know that your life has great meaning.

Significance is when you know and understand the reason why you are here on planet Earth.

Chapter Two

KNOWING YOUR REAL IDENTITY

One of the greatest problems facing humanity is that people do not know their real identity. Your identity serves as a reference point that directs the course of your life. It is a compass that provides direction for every area of your life. It connects you with your origin and your purpose.

Knowing your true identity is a pre-requisite to fulfilling your destiny. Life's decisions are made based on who you think you are. Your thoughts and decisions cannot go beyond the perspective that you have of self.

Your thoughts and decisions cannot go beyond the perspective that you have of self.

Whenever our self-identity is based upon incomplete knowledge of self, we live substandard and unfruitful lives outside of the Will of God.

My childhood theory of being dropped off by angels was comforting and for a long time I rested in that assumption. That theory was good as long as I was willing to remain in ignorance. Hell's strategy is to keep you ignorant so you will never know who you are or your pre-natal assignment. Self-discovery demands that you embrace truth and reject lies. I came to a realization that if I was to find out the truth about me, I would have to search beyond myself.

Every day you hear about different discoveries that are being made. God has prospered the minds of so many to pioneer and discover so much. But, the greatest discovery that anyone could ever make is self-discovery. When you discover self, you come into a knowledge of your true identity. There is no greater discovery than that. It is impossible to discover self without first discovering God.

It is impossible to discover self without first discovering God.

God is the source of all truth and, without knowing Him, you will live a life based on lies. To know your pre-natal assignment, you must know God.

You have to be connected to the source of your life. Your entrance into this world and even your conception was because God allowed it. Your identity originated in God and was designed by God. He foreordained your existence. He foreknew me—He foreknew you. He governs, dictates, upholds, and sanctions all things according to His will and purpose.

I read and studied the writings of many of the great philosophers and even professed to be a follower. However, there was still that tugging and that yearning for the truth. None of those that I followed was able to give me a full understanding of my true identity. Nothing that I read, nor any of these philosophers, presented anything to me that gave me a full understanding of who I was from God's perspective. I was still locked in an abyss of ignorance regarding my true identity.

It was not until I had surrendered my life to the greatest Liberator of all times, the Lord Jesus Christ that I was able to find out the truth about me. In order to know what my pre-natal assignment was, I had to develop a personal relationship with the One who gives the assignment. I first had to learn the truth about Him. I had to learn that He is the Source of all life.

I came to know and understand the true meaning of source. I kept looking to man as a source of truth and knowledge about me, but it wasn't until I came to know my God as my real Father, that I was able to tap into the significance of my genesis and the purpose of my life.

When I accepted Jesus as my personal Lord and Savior, I came to realize that, spiritually, I was not an orphan and God Himself is my Father. I learned that my life was established by Him and through Him from the beginning. I realized that my life was hid in Him and to find out the truth about me, I had to go through Him. In Him I found my true identity.

A ship without a compass gets lost in the ocean and is subject to devastating waves and ends up in destructive channels and ports that are so far away from its destination. Life without true understanding of your identity is like that ship on the ocean that is without any real direction.

The most terrible form of ignorance is when you do not know who you are from God's perspective. When you live with this form of ignorance, you open up yourself for the devil to control the thoughts you have toward self. Self-hatred, low self-esteem, and self-condemnation are typical signs of those who have no concept of their true identity. Many people suffer from severe pain and exist in a quagmire of hopelessness because of such ignorance. Instead of leading productive lives, they are infected by negativity and pervasive thoughts that breed devastation and despair.

These are spiritual maladies and can only be treated with spiritual medicine. The Word of God is medicine for your soul. God's Word opens up your eyes to who you really are and it defines your identity.

1 Peter 2:9 (KJV)

9 But ye are a chosen generation, a royal priesthood, an holy nation, a peculiar people; that ye should shew forth the praises of him who hath called you out of darkness into his marvellous light:

You are not an accident. Your birth was not a mistake or a mishap. Your life is not a fluke of nature. Your parents might not have planned you, but God did. Your parents might have been surprised by your birth but God was not. As a matter of fact, He fully expected it.

According to the Bible, God ordained Jeremiah to be a Prophet before he was born. Well, let it be known, God's sovereignty is not just partial to Jeremiah. Before you were born, you too were ordained to occupy a particular office here on earth. God told Jeremiah that He sanctified him. That means he was set apart for a particular thing to do for God. He was especially made for something and so were you.

Like so many people, Jeremiah was ignorant of his worth and his purpose. The voice of God, with all the authority of heaven, announced to Jeremiah his extraordinary worth. The pages of this book, prophetically announce to you that your worth is inseparably tied to the truth that you were made by God, for God. You were made in His image and after His likeness which authenticates your lineage.

It will bring great honor to God if you would see yourself as He sees you. No longer should you see yourself negatively:

- I am a misfit.

- I am nothing.

- I am no good.

- I am ugly.

- I don't have what it takes.

- I am not important.

- I am too this and too that.

You need to know that you are wonderfully and fearfully made. God supervised *"your before-birth"* and if you allow Him, He will continue the job even after birth. He numbered your days before you were born. Just like He put the stars in the sky, God orchestrated every single detail of your creation. He deliberately chose your race, the color of your skin, the color of your eyes, even the number of hairs on your head.

The Bible declares to us that we are God's workmanship created in Christ Jesus for good works. It also tells us that these good works were prepared beforehand that we should walk in them.

Ephesians 2:10 (KJV)

10 For we are his workmanship, created in Christ Jesus unto good works, which God hath before ordained that we should walk in them.

This verse of scripture is so revealing because it defines who we are. It tells us that we are created in Christ Jesus which means that the source of our DNA is found in Christ. You are a part of God. This gives us a clear picture of how biology serves to facilitate what God has spiritually ordained. Just think, millions of sperm fought to make their way to your mother's egg. You, with your dynamic personality, made your way to that egg. You wiggled your way in. Right at that moment, the outer wall of the ovum changed its chemical composition and shut tight, sealing the entrance.

The source of our DNA is found in Christ.

You were a conqueror from the beginning. From the very beginning you were determined and purpose-driven. Even when you were a tiny speck, you knew how to press your way to victory. You were a winner from the beginning. You started out with so many other sperm, but you were the only one that God allowed to make it. You beat the odds because you were destined to be here. You could have died, unborn, but here you are a testimony to God's sovereignty.

Babies are tagged at birth to preserve their identity. And Guess what? You were tagged before you were born with your identity. You were tagged before birth with your real identity for Kingdom purpose. Some were tagged to be Teachers, Pastors, Evangelists, Prophets, and Apostles. There was a spiritual impartation and empowerment that was released into your spirit man before you were born.

Before you were born, you were only spirit. God transported the spirit man (male and female) by way of a sperm that fertilized an egg in the womb of the natural man (female). Conception took place and you were incubated throughout a nine month process of growth and development. After nine months, you were birthed into the earth realm. Your spirit man was encased in the body of a boy or a girl. Even though you were tagged before birth, your purpose has never left you and you are expected to carry out the pre-natal assignment on your life. You were tagged with a pre-natal assignment in eternity. God transported you out of eternity, via your father, into your mother's womb.

You were tagged with a pre-natal assignment in eternity.

When God spoke to Jeremiah and said, "before I formed thee . . ." So much was said in that one statement. The *before* validates, authenticates, and substantiates that you have purpose and that you are supposed to be.

When you have an understanding of your true identity, you will begin to soar like the eagle. You will begin to celebrate your life with passion and conviction of purpose. Taking hold of your true identity is paramount in carrying out your pre-natal assignment. So many people spend hundreds of dollars pursuing the wrong career and a college education that has nothing to do with their pre-natal assignment. Let God define who you are and let His Word build you up and strengthen you to complete your assignment.

Chapter Three

WHAT IS MY ASSIGNMENT HERE?

God released you into the earth realm with a specific assignment for you to accomplish on this planet. You did not come here haphazardly. Your arrival on earth was a deliberate act of God. You came pre-packaged with gifts and talents to carry out your assignment. The wonderful thing about this assignment is that God, Himself, ordained you for this task. You have been wired with "God" stuff.

Everything about you was meticulously shaped and formed. As a matter of fact, your stuff is of the highest value because it came directly from God. You reflect the magnificence of God. Wow, just think about that! The very breath that you breathe is God's breath.

Your capacity to succeed is voluminous. You were not made on an assembly line. Everything about you was carefully and wonderfully designed by God. When God considered excellence, you were in His mind.

Genesis 1:26-28 (KJV)

26 And God said, Let us make man in our image, after our likeness: and let them have dominion

*over the fish of the sea, and over the fowl of the
air, and over the cattle, and over all the earth, and
over every creeping thing that creepeth upon the
earth.*

*27 So God created man in his own image, in the
image of God created he him; male and female
created he them.*

*28 And God blessed them, and God said unto them,
Be fruitful, and multiply, and replenish the earth,
and subdue it: and have dominion over the fish
of the sea, and over the fowl of the air, and over
every living thing that moveth upon the earth.*

Your pre-natal assignment is tied to the dominion mandate. You are designed to be fruitful. You were made to be a multiplier. Deeply rooted in your innermost being is the ability to replenish this earth and use all of its resources to the honor and glory of God.

God does not make junk and God made you good. In fact, He made you very good. There is nothing about you that God did not consider. Not only were you made by God, but you were made to be a functional being capable of reaching great heights and excelling in everything you do. Inside of you is a network of creative excellence that is designed to facilitate your pre-natal assignment from God.

Jeremiah's pre-natal assignment was to be a prophet to the nations. God gave him whatever he needed to accommodate the assignment. Before he was born, God had supernaturally deposited things in him that would enable him to rule over nations and kingdoms. His seed was deposited in his mother's womb, fully loaded with the potential to pull down, throw down, and destroy principalities that were established against the Kingdom of God. Before Jeremiah was formed in his mother's womb, God had meticulously placed an appreciation for building and planting in his soul.

Jeremiah 1:6-10 (KJV)

6 Then said I, Ah, Lord GOD! behold, I cannot speak: for I am a child.

7 But the LORD said unto me, Say not, I am a child: for thou shalt go to all that I shall send thee, and whatsoever I command thee thou shalt speak.

8 Be not afraid of their faces: for I am with thee to deliver thee, saith the LORD.

9 Then the LORD put forth his hand, and touched my mouth. And the LORD said unto me, Behold, I have put my words in thy mouth.

10 See, I have this day set thee over the nations and over the kingdoms, to root out, and to pull down, and to destroy, and to throw down, to build, and to plant.

So many people are ignorant of God's purpose for their lives and they live a life of pain and disappointment that ends in failure. They are completely oblivious to what their existence here on earth is all about. They wake up every morning and they go to sleep every night or, in many cases, spend sleepless nights wondering what is the meaning of life.

A broken clock on the wall serves no purpose. You will never know what time of day it is if your only barometer of time is a broken clock. Time is the currency by which purpose is obtained. How you spend your time provides a summary of your life achievements. Ignorance of your pre-natal assignment is just like the broken clock—it defeats purpose.

Ignorance of your pre-natal assignment is just like the broken clock—it defeats purpose.

The vast majority of earth's inhabitants live unfulfilled lives and they die in a state of unfulfillment. Every day, you meet people hustling and bustling on the subway, strolling in the shopping malls, or sitting at their desks at work, who have no idea of their significance in the plan of God. Some of these people wish they could do better and do more with their lives, but they never see themselves as being able to pursue dreams and change their present state.

Their lives encompass broken dreams and their vocabulary sends messages of "I wish I could, but I can't." So many accept mediocrity and they settle for anything. One of the things I learned early in life is, "If you don't know where you are going you can end up anywhere."

If you don't know where you are going, you can end up anywhere.

One of the saddest things to behold is a person standing at the traffic light with a sign saying "God bless you" and their hands are stretched out for whatever you willingly or unwillingly give to them. The sign says "God bless you" but yet they do not recognize that they, too, are blessed by God with wonderful gifts and talents. They see poverty as their portion and like the broken clock on the wall, they are dysfunctional and exist in a world of non-productivity.

So many were born who lived and died without depositing anything into this earth. History has nothing to show that they ever existed. The only trace of their lives is a tombstone which testifies to the fact that their gifts and talents were buried with them.

For me, life had to have meaning. I was not comfortable with just a meager existence of being able to pay the rent and put food in the refrigerator. Buying clothes and having money to splurge here and there was just not enough for me. I was burdened with a deep desire to know the purpose of my life here on earth and "why the angels dropped me off on this planet."

One of the greatest reference manuals that we have access to is the Bible. It provides answers and wisdom that teaches us about anything that we would ever want to know. The manuscript of this great book gives a plethora of answers that leads to an understanding of who you really are and provides fundamental truths for self-discovery.

Ephesians 2:10 (KJV)

10 For we are his workmanship, created in Christ Jesus unto good works, which God hath before ordained that we should walk in them.

Many people lead unproductive and unfulfilled lives without any real purpose and meaning beyond the instant and short-lived gratification of material things such as money, sex, power, and the temporal attachments of accolades that have no real meaning.

But life bears more meaning than these mundane eventualities and within each of us there are gifts and talents that have not yet been discovered and are waiting to be activated. God, in His divine wisdom, has endowed us with the tools to live a life of real significance and purpose.

All of us have general assignments from God. However, each of us is individually tagged with a specific assignment that is consistent with our divine purpose. We are all born to give God praise and to worship Him. Our lives should be an uninterrupted hallelujah chorus of praise—and worship is to be our trademark.

Our lives should be an uninterrupted hallelujah chorus of praise—and worship is to be our trademark.

Nonetheless, beyond the general assignment is the pre-natal assignment that you have been given to complete in the earth. The effect of this assignment, if carried out, would leave a legacy in the earth and change lives forever.

You might be at a place in your life where it seems as though death is better. The truth of the matter is that not living in purpose is death itself. Even though you are breathing and physically alive, you are spiritually dead. You are the living dead when you are disconnected from God's purpose for your life. There is something on the inside of you for you to use to the honor and glory of God. There are books and songs in many of us. God did not send you here to meander through life without purpose or direction.

There is more to you than what you see with your natural eyes. There is greatness on the inside of you. You can be that preacher. You can be that doctor. You can be that evangelist covering the globe with the Gospel of the Kingdom. You can be that teacher or that designer. You can write several best-selling books. God has placed creativity on the inside of you. You were made in His image and after His likeness. You can use your gifts and talents to create masterpieces and move out of your present state into God's plan for your life. You do not have to settle for mediocrity and life at the bottom.

You do not have to settle for mediocrity and life at the bottom.

Deuteronomy 28:13 (KJV)

13 And the LORD shall make thee the head, and not the tail; and thou shalt be above only, and thou shalt not be beneath;

Before you were even conceived in your mother's womb, the Triune Godhead had a board meeting about you. At this meeting, The Board of Triune Counsel came to an agreement that you and I would be so special that we would have the genetic coding which would enable us to represent God through our gifts and talents.

Just imagine, a Holy God, the CEO of Heaven and earth, makes such a sovereign administrative decision to create you and to create me. And then, saw it fit to endow us with great capacity to dominate the earth.

Genesis 1:26 (KJV)

26 And God said, Let us make man in our image, after our likeness: and let them have dominion over the fish of the sea, and over the fowl of the air, and over the cattle, and over all the earth, and over every creeping thing that creepeth upon the earth.

God bestowed upon man the privilege and the right to act on His behalf. Whatever role God saw fit that we should execute on behalf of His Kingdom here on earth, He released an executive blessing upon man to do so. The blessing included a benefit package that was all sufficient for man (male and female) to have dominion.

This special blessing was a seal of authenticity. When you are authentic, it means you have an inalienable right to utilize the uniqueness of your character to represent God. Your authenticity governs your capabilities and is reflected in the way you instinctively conduct yourself.

- You are not a bird—that is why you do not fly.

- You are not a cow—that is why you do not moo and chew your cud.

- You are not a cat—that is why you do not purr.

- You are not a dog—that is why you do not bark and wag your tail

Just like the bird, the cow, the cat, and the dog, God has blessed you with gifts and talents for you to use that will bring Him glory. Every gift and talent that you possess is tied to the pre-natal assignment on your life.

Chapter Four

THE JOURNEY

Your pre-natal assignment is tied to your prophetic destiny. In His sovereign Will, God gave you an assignment for His Kingdom purpose. The earth is in the hand of God and He has sovereign authority over all that He has created. Before each seed is deposited in the womb of a woman, God divinely declares its purpose and He sanctions an assignment for the life of each person. No one is born without a pre-natal assignment. That is why He was able to talk to the Prophet Jeremiah the way He did.

Jeremiah 1:4-10 (KJV)

4 Then the word of the LORD came unto me, saying,

5 Before I formed thee in the belly I knew thee; and before thou camest forth out of the womb I sanctified thee, and I ordained thee a prophet unto the nations.

6 Then said I, Ah, Lord GOD! behold, I cannot speak: for I am a child.

7 But the LORD said unto me, Say not, I am a child: for thou shalt go to all that I shall send thee, and whatsoever I command thee thou shalt speak.

8 Be not afraid of their faces: for I am with thee to deliver thee, saith the LORD.

9 Then the LORD put forth his hand, and touched my mouth. And the LORD said unto me, Behold, I have put my words in thy mouth.

10 See, I have this day set thee over the nations and over the kingdoms, to root out, and to pull down, and to destroy, and to throw down, to build, and to plant.

Your destiny is tied to your assignment. However, far too many are unable to step into their destiny because they suffer from past wounds that have never healed. The view of the future can be dimmed by circumstances of the past. When most of your time is spent looking in the rear view mirror instead of in front of you, it is very difficult to move forward. The excruciating pain of past wounds has crushed and broken you so badly that you are left in a never-ending spiral of sorrow and despair. Paralysis sets in and moving forward is seemingly impossible.

Most people have not grasped the idea that crushing, although painful, can be a great blessing. A grape can only produce wine after it has been crushed. The fragrance of a rose is heightened after it has been crushed. A diamond only glistens after it has been cut. The beauty of pure gold is only seen after it has gone through the fire. So, the crushing of yesterday serves to push you into your prophetic destiny.

Most people have not grasped the idea that crushing, although painful, can be a great blessing.

Here is a revelation: The greatness that lies within you can only come forth after the crushing. Olive oil is produced by grinding and crushing whole olives until the oil is extracted. Life's circumstance is like an olive press that crushes you until the virgin oil of God's glory seeps out of you and the sweet-smelling savor of His presence saturates you. None of us is exempt from pain and suffering. Even those who live Godly, the Bible assures us of our portion of suffering.

2 Timothy 3:12 (KJV)

12 Yea, and all that will live godly in Christ Jesus shall suffer persecution.

The Bible gives examples of men and women who were crushed by the circumstances of life, but yet they prevailed as more than conquerors and stepped into their destiny. The journey to your destiny favors crushing that will propel you to heights of victory and dominion, which would otherwise escape you. Stop for a minute and give God thanks for the crushing!

The journey to your destiny favors crushing that will propel you to heights of victory and dominion, which would otherwise escape you.

Due to a lack of understanding and discernment, many reject what God is trying to do in their lives during a season of crushing. You rebuke your blessing and you label it as a work of satan when God is putting you through the process of transformation. We must change the confessions of our mouths so we do not self-destruct.

Proverbs 18:21 (KJV)

Death and life are in the power of the tongue: and they that love it shall eat the fruit thereof.

Oftentimes, we see that the greater the crushing, the greater the elevation. Endurance in such times allows us to defy the gravitational pull that would keep our minds locked down in a cesspool of bitterness, hatred, and resentment. All of the above are destiny-blockers and should be avoided at any cost.

Let's look at some Biblical examples of people who were able to endure the crushing process and move into their prophetic destiny.

Before Abraham rose to prominence, he and Sarah were crushed with many years without a child.

Before Jacob could be blessed, his crushing came by way of being crippled in a wrestling match with God.

Before Joseph became the Prime Minister of Egypt, his personal crushing came via a pit, slavery, and prison.

Before Moses became the great deliverer, he was crushed by losing his palace position, his possessions, and his status.

Before Job's estate was doubled, he was crushed by losing all his possessions and his family.

Before Joshua conquered the Promised Land, he was crushed through the wilderness.

They had to be crushed to bring out what was in them. Crushing is a prerequisite to greatness.

It breaks us into what God requires of us. Just like the process of extracting oil from the olives is done through crushing and pressing, we have to be pressed and crushed to bring out what is in us. During this process there is a separation that is necessary to produce oil. There must be a separation from people, places, and things that would prevent the oil from flowing.

Crushing is a prerequisite to greatness.

The journey to your destiny is punctuated by circumstances which will press and crush you until God gets all that He wants out of you. Pre-natal assignments always include an encounter with the "olive press."

Psalm 51:17 (KJV)

17 The sacrifices of God are a broken spirit: a broken and a contrite heart, O God, thou wilt not despise.

The journey lies ahead of you. And, unless you bury the past, you will never finish the race to cross over into your prophetic destiny. Moving toward your prophetic destiny means that you have to keep looking at what is before you and not what is behind. The Apostle Paul understood that his past was not his future and he had to let go of his past in order to obtain the prize.

The pre-natal assignment that God has mandated for each of our lives demands that we press our way to completion.

Philippians 3:13-14 (KJV)

13 Brethren, I count not myself to have apprehended: but this one thing I do, forgetting

29

those things which are behind, and reaching forth unto those things which are before,

14 I press toward the mark for the prize of the high calling of God in Christ Jesus.

Pre-natal assignments always include an encounter with the "olive press."

Chapter Five

CONFRONTING THE WOUNDS AND UNVEILING THE SCARS

Undoubtedly, all of us can relate to the subject of wounds and scars. So many people have not been able to understand the great motivator called pain. The value of pain has been grossly devalued and it is not regarded as a destiny propeller. Many give up on the pre-natal assignment that God has given them because they see pain as an enemy and not as a positive force in their lives.

In my own life, I had to make a concerted effort to "kill" the wounds and bury them. I had to protect my mind from recurring images of the past that would put me in a state of paralysis. After many years of living in the past and rehashing painful memories, I decided to adopt the attitude of the Apostle Paul to leave those things behind, permanently. As long as I wallowed in self-pity and allowed my soul to be overwhelmed by the pain of wounds, that were inflicted by self or other people, I was giving the enemy permission to control my mind and my destiny.

Burying the wounds alive proved to be a futile attempt in mind management and liberation. The only real mind management I could employ was to confront the pain of these wounds and render it lifeless. I learned a long time ago that where there is no confrontation, there is no resolution. I made a decision that I would no longer give the wounds of my past permission to dictate the state of my mind and navigate the path of my future.

Confrontation is more than just acknowledging that the pain exists. It is going to the source and cutting off its life support. In confronting the root of your pain, you are challenged to first confront self and to forgive self. It requires that you take the high road and forgive those who were the perpetrators of your pain.

_____

In confronting the root of your pain, you are challenged to first confront self and to forgive self.

_____

The process of confrontation, for many people, has its own timeline. True deliverance comes only when you are ready to be delivered. It comes when you are truly sick and tired of your present circumstance and you make a decision to welcome change.

Whenever pain is swept under the rug and hidden in the recesses of the mind, it becomes a stumbling block rather than a strengthening life-lesson. Many painful issues have been buried but they were never dead. As a result, many are haunted by vivid memories and are attacked by skeletons from the grave. The memories present themselves at times when they are least expected—late in the midnight hour, sitting up in church, alone at home, anywhere, and at anytime.

Self-medication has been administered and it appears as though healing has taken place. There have even been scabs but, underneath, the wounds have not been healed and years later you realize the matter has never been settled. The issue was buried, but it was not dead.

As a result, we carry the scars as lingering signs of mental or physical injury. The scars serve to remind us of damages and blemishes from some former attachment. For many of us, the wounds are self-inflicted and we are left with guilt and shame that block us from carrying out God's pre-natal assignment for our lives.

Psalm 38:5-6 (KJV)

5 My wounds stink and are corrupt because of my foolishness.

6 I am troubled; I am bowed down greatly; I go mourning all the day long.

Some wounds are the result of unpleasant experiences that have been unleashed on us through no fault of our own. Many suffer from the painful experience of damaging words coupled with physical and mental abuse. Others have been subjugated to rejection, violation, and betrayal that have left them paralyzed and dysfunctional.

The bottom line is that all wounds deliver pain and can cause us to malfunction. These wounds have become a silent partner to so many and have been crutches for those who have accepted the devil's plan of failure and defeat. That is why we see so many precious people in and out of the church whose lives are overcome by lethargy, slothfulness, double-mindedness, and indifference.

The devil's plan is to keep you from converting pain to purpose. You become so attached to the pain that it becomes a crutch and an excuse not to move forward but to remain in a state of unproductivity.

John 10:10 (KJV)

10 The thief cometh not, but for to steal, and to kill, and to destroy: I am come that they might have life, and that they might have it more abundantly.

For some, confrontation never takes place and so much time is spent on nursing the wounds—morning time, noon time, evening time, night time. The same pain that you went to bed with last night is the same pain that is your companion tonight and that same pain is your alarm clock that ushers you into another day. You go through another day not being able to focus, not being able to do anything right, not being able to make any positive impact on the world because you have given past wounds and the present pain the authority to govern your life.

These wounds go beyond our physical bodies and inflict deep injury to the faculties of the soul—intellect, will, desire, imagination, and emotion. Wounding that takes place in the unseen area of our beings is concealed but it is damaging just the same. These wounds leave negative effects upon our lives and manifest in self-destructive attitudes and behaviors. Victims of these wounds remain unmotivated, fearful, and tormented. They exist from day to day while the pre-natal assignment on their lives is unrecognized and unappreciated. They remain locked up in strongholds such as:

- Inferiority complex—never feeling good about themselves and never thinking they can measure up.

- Stubbornness—locked in the vain imaginations of their minds. They become suspicious, distrustful, and unforgiving. They are locked in, hemmed up, shut down, oppressed, and depressed.

It is important to understand that your appointment with your destiny might come by way of wounding. Though it might bring great pain, you must know that your healing has already taken place in the spiritual realm and your faith in God will bring an open manifestation.

It is important to understand that your appointment with your destiny might come by way of wounding.

In spite of daily challenges, we must never see ourselves as defeated. God has made us to be overcomers. The Bible declares that we are more than conquerors. Our Heavenly Father loves us even when we are dealing with the wounds and because of His great love for us, He stands ready to heal us.

Romans 8:37-39 (KJV)

37 Nay, in all these things we are more than conquerors through him that loved us.

38 For I am persuaded, that neither death, nor life, nor angels, nor principalities, nor powers, nor things present, nor things to come,

39 Nor height, nor depth, nor any other creature, shall be able to separate us from the love of God, which is in Christ Jesus our Lord.

As you are reading the pages of this book, I invite you to join me and really take a look at these wounds. I want you to confront the pain and unveil the scars. That means some of you will have to take a walk through the graveyard—the graveyard of your mind. We will have to go into the subconscious mind—the hard drive—the data control.

There are some things that you have buried but they are not dead and you need to exhume them so that you can kill them once and for all. They were buried alive and they still call you from the grave. The constant graveyard call is blocking you from carrying out the pre-natal assignment on your lives. You buried the abortion, but it is not dead. You cannot live with the memory of that self-inflected wound.

You buried the rape, but it is not dead. That is why you wake up every day to excruciating pain in your soul and you cry secret tears as you deal with the pain and suffering. You become hunched over, burdened down, engrossed in pain as you aimlessly crawl through life. You buried it, but it is not dead.

Proverbs 18:14 (KJV)

14 The spirit of a man will sustain his infirmity; but a wounded spirit who can bear?

A wound that is not healed creates a void for satan to fill. The Bible declares that a wounded spirit is worse than physical sickness. Physical illness can be sustained by a healthy spirit but a sick spirit cannot be healed by anything in the natural. You can suffer from a car accident, a broken limb, a fractured skull and recover easily but, if your spirit is wounded, how can you cope? If you feel like a nobody, if your mind is messed up and depressed, if you feel as though life is worthless, if you are numb and have no feelings, it is impossible to pursue God's purpose for your life.

No matter how healthy you might look, if the spirit is wounded, you cannot and will not operate as a healthy person.

A wound that is not healed creates a void for satan to fill.

Proverbs 17:22 (KJV)

22 A merry heart doeth good like a medicine: but a broken spirit drieth the bones.

Many of us have suffered from wounds, bruises, and putrefying sores. So many people wake up each morning, barely clinging to the shirttails of life because all they have to live for is a new day of torture from wounds that have not healed. They live lives in desolate places and they suffer in silence void of any awareness of their pre-natal assignment.

Isaiah 1:6 (KJV)

6 From the sole of the foot even unto the head there is no soundness in it; but wounds, and bruises, and putrifying sores: they have not been closed, neither bound up, neither mollified with ointment.

Until you learn how to use the pain to facilitate gain, you will never be able to maximize your full potential and execute your pre-natal assignment from God. You have to choose to kill the wounds and bury them. You have to get to a place of real departure from the wounds of the past so you can enter into the newness of life with Christ. You have to put to death those crippling memories and bury them once and for all. For too long they have been buried alive and they keep calling from the grave. When we hold on to the wounds that have been inflicted upon us, we commit our lives to a state of desolation and we never get out of the crisis mode.

When we hold on to the wounds that have been inflicted upon us, we commit our lives to a state of desolation and we never get out of the crisis mode.

In the Bible, we see where Tamar did not release herself from the devastating wounds of deceit, rape, and rejection. The violation left her desolate and subverted her pre-natal assignment. Instead, her life's story serves as an example of pain and suffering that was never converted to success and fulfillment.

2 Samuel 13:14-20 (KJV)

[14] Howbeit he would not hearken unto her voice: but, being stronger than she, forced her, and lay with her.

[15] Then Amnon hated her exceedingly; so that the hatred wherewith he hated her was greater than the love wherewith he had loved her. And Amnon said unto her, Arise, be gone.

[16] And she said unto him, There is no cause: this evil in sending me away is greater than the other that thou didst unto me. But he would not hearken unto her.

[17] Then he called his servant that ministered unto him, and said, Put now this woman out from me, and bolt the door after her.

[18] And she had a garment of divers colours upon her: for with such robes were the king's daughters

*that were virgins apparelled. Then his servant
brought her out, and bolted the door after her.*

*¹⁹ And Tamar put ashes on her head, and rent her
garment of divers colours that was on her, and laid
her hand on her head, and went on crying.*

*²⁰ And Absalom her brother said unto her, Hath
Amnon thy brother been with thee? but hold now
thy peace, my sister: he is thy brother; regard
not this thing. So Tamar remained desolate in her
brother Absalom's house.*

So many people suffer from the same malady that possessed Tamar. In silence they suffer, and suffer, and suffer. These are the wounded spirits of the world. They are on our jobs; they are our neighbors; they are in our churches; they are in our homes. I can imagine the terror that Tamar faced. Daily, she lived with the wounds of her experience and settled for a life of desolation. Oh, how she must have lived the rape a "zillion" times each day. Hopeless and non-trusting she chose to die while she was yet breathing.

It is the desire of my heart that those of you, who have been shattered by the same wounds as Tamar, will finally get a release from the pain and suffering. The words on these pages serve as a catharsis for deliverance and healing.

You have been wounded, broken, and betrayed. The rape, the incest, the abuse, and the molestation, as painful as they are to remember, serve to make you stronger. You can emerge from this experience with a greater strength and a greater resolve to press on and complete your pre-natal assignment.

Look at Job. What pain and suffering he must have experienced, but he was made better for the pain of going through. Yes, he was crushed but, at the end of the day, he stood as more than a conqueror and regained everything he lost.

Job 42:12 (KJV)

12 So the LORD blessed the latter end of Job more than his beginning: for he had fourteen thousand sheep, and six thousand camels, and a thousand yoke of oxen, and a thousand she asses.

Some of you have been emotionally crippled and are now limping. You are hoping for a miracle. You want to be whole again. But before you can straighten up and walk tall and begin to function as God would have you to function, you must be delivered from the effects of past wounds.

Challenge yourself today. Make a resolve to put the pain to death and bury it permanently. Your prophetic destiny is calling you.

Some of us have suffered some wounds and were left with scars that hold us hostage to our past. Apathy, anger, bitterness, self-hatred, and suicidal thoughts are all symptoms of wounds that have been buried alive. True healing has to take place on the inside. Burying the wounds alive only leaves you patched up but not healed. Some people think that they can just press CTRL+ ALT+ Delete and their wounds will disappear.

True healing has to take place on the inside.

Some of you have been crushed with some things that have left you with pain that is so hard to live with and, as a result, you pretend as though they never happened.

You live a life of cover up. You try to fake out people by acting like you are OK but deep down you are unsettled and you are hanging on by a thin thread. As a result, you are not operating at your optimal level in Christ. You look to the opiates to deal with the wounds that are oozing. You choose your drug of choice: cocaine, alcohol, food, cigarettes, sex, people, etc. You take these drugs hoping to get a permanent fix but you end up with only temporary remedies. You keep seeking "a fix" and going back for more but healing never takes place. You have to kill it once and for all.

Today, I need you to declare with all boldness and confidence that you are healed! Say these words, **"I am healed and delivered in the name of Jesus."** Keep saying that until it resonates so deeply in your heart and mind that your actions will correspond with what is in your soul.

Exodus 15:21 (KJV)

I am the Lord thy God that healeth thee;

May I recommend to you the greatest physician of all times? He has a perfect track record and He has never lost a patient. Go see the physician, Dr. Jesus. His medical name is Jehovah Rapha. He is also known as the Balm in Gilead. Put yourself in a position to get your healing. His prescription guarantees a true conversion. Whatever is your deficiency or ailment—mental, physical, emotional or spiritual, Dr. Jesus can heal you.

A true conversion heals the wounds. When true healing takes place, you will be ready to carry out your pre-natal assignment and you can be used in ministry.

Yes, there is a balm in Gilead—there is a physician in the house and He specializes in sin-sick souls. You do not even need an appointment with Dr. Jesus. His office is open to walk-ins. You do not have to worry about an insurance card and satisfying a deductible is not necessary. There is no co-pay and no waiting period. You can see Him at any time—day or night.

Isaiah 61:1-3 (KJV)

1 The Spirit of the Lord GOD is upon me; because the LORD hath anointed me to preach good tidings unto the meek; he hath sent me to bind up the brokenhearted, to proclaim liberty to the captives, and the opening of the prison to them that are bound;

2 To proclaim the acceptable year of the LORD, and the day of vengeance of our God; to comfort all that mourn;

3 To appoint unto them that mourn in Zion, to give unto them beauty for ashes, the oil of joy for mourning, the garment of praise for the spirit of heaviness; that they might be called trees of righteousness, the planting of the LORD, that he might be glorified.

Arise, people of destiny! Get up off the canvas and move on to conquer great things. Your pre-natal assignment awaits you.

Psalm 147:3 (KJV)

He healeth the broken heart and bindedth up their wounds.

Jeremiah 30:17 (KJV)

For I will restore health unto thee, and I will heal thee of thy wounds.

Chapter Six

ROADBLOCKS TO YOUR DESTINY

It is amazing how many people do not understand that the pre-natal assignment is to be executed within the bounds of God's Kingdom here on earth. Whatever pre-natal assignment we have been given has been sanctioned by God and it carries a Kingdom mandate. You are destined for a place in the Kingdom of God.

The most important thing for us, as believers and even unbelievers, is to understand that we have a destiny. Destiny demands that you focus on your assignment and avoid the adversarial roadblocks that have been directed from hell against you. A person who is cognizant of destiny is a person who recognizes the urgency of "**pressing toward the mark.**"

Press! Press! Press!

Philippians 3:13-14 (KJV)

13 Brethren, I count not myself to have apprehended: but this one thing I do, forgetting those things which are behind, and reaching forth unto those things which are before,

14 I press toward the mark for the prize of the high calling of God in Christ Jesus.

Destiny demands that you focus on your assignment and avoid the adversarial roadblocks that have been directed from hell against you.

It is easy to get lost and confused if you are not focused. Too many people are missing the mark and are meandering through life without any purpose or direction. Even people sitting up in churches are lost and exist in a quagmire of derailment and confusion. Lost, meaning they have come off the main road that leads to their destiny. They find themselves on some back road that leads them to nowhere and they are floating through life with no purpose.

If you do not embrace your destiny, it means you have not embraced purpose. Life without purpose is a life without meaning. The Bible declares that a man's life does not consist of things he possesses. It is not about the things that you have. It is about living the life that God has designed and destined for you to live. With all your possessions and with all your stuff, where does that put you if you have gained everything and lost your soul.

Life without purpose is a life without meaning.

Many people give the appearance of a life that is on track but are merely faking it until they make it. Yes, they are dressed up every Sunday and look like they are going somewhere but they are off course and need to make a U-Turn. Unfortunately, when it comes to executing and carrying out your pre-natal assignment, pretense is not an an option. Pretense puts you outside of the Will of God and you set yourself on a course of self-destruction.

Pretense puts you outside of the Will of God and you set yourself on a course of self-destruction.

Whenever you find you have missed God, don't sit around and wallow in confusion. Here are three simple things you can do: disengage promptly, recover quickly, and advance in a new direction. In other words, stop, get yourself together, and get on the right track. You cannot make a right turn if you are in the wrong lane. Make a "U-Turn" quickly.

God's plan for you and me is that we should carry out our pre-natal assignment in such a way that we empty ourselves of everything He has placed on the inside of us. We should pour out our gifts and talents in the Kingdom of God. Leaving this earth empty and not full can only be accomplished when we carry out our pre-natal assignment. Too many people leave this earth full and have never emptied themselves of projects and so much more that was designed to benefit the Kingdom of God here on earth. The greatest accomplishment that a person can achieve is to die empty and not full.

Leaving this earth empty and not full can only be accomplished when we carry out our pre-natal assignment.

When you look around and see so much perversion and how things are crisscrossed and turned upside down, you realize the state of urgency in which we live. Everything that was wrong has now been accepted as right and the right is now wrong. People have lost sight of destiny and they have put God out of the equation and are now operating with a new math. Things are not adding up and yet they are trying to make a square peg fit into a round hole.

Even in the churches, there is a new kind of rhetoric and church folk are now accepting man's law instead of God's Word. God is looking for a people who are not willing to accept societal norms, but are destiny-driven. They understand their role in the Kingdom and are willing to pursue it.

- Nothing can make them waiver.

- Nothing can hold them back.

- Nothing can make them quit.

- Nothing can make them retreat.

They will allow nothing to deter them from pursuing their destiny.

God has a specific plan for your life. Not one detail concerning your destiny has been overlooked. God knows the beginning, the middle and the end of your life. He has already drafted the blue print. He has set the course that you should take. There might be some stops along the way but, if you allow God, He will lead you to where you ought to be. You just have to circumvent the roadblocks from hell that try to derail you and cause you to get off course.

God knows the beginning, the middle and the end of your life. He has already drafted the blue print.

There is a story in the Bible, in the book of Judges, the sixteenth chapter. This story is about a man who had a pre-natal assignment but experienced great roadblocks to his destiny. Samson was a Nazarite. That means he was set apart and dedicated only for the use of God. The presence of God was upon his life in a very special way. Samson was appointed to be a judge, one of the deliverers of Israel. He had been called by God to a very special ministry. But, from the very beginning of adulthood, his private life was a disaster. Women became his downfall.

Samson was inconsistent throughout his entire life. He chose to live an illicit life of sin that did not glorify God. The presence of sin in Samson's life was a major roadblock to his destiny. A man who was born to accomplish such great feats for Israel lost his power and ability because of a sinful life. The loss of God's presence is a major roadblock to your destiny.

The loss of God's presence is a major roadblock to your destiny.

Without the presence of God you lose so much.

- Samson lost his vision.

- Samson lost his dominion.

- Samson lost his status.

- Samson lost his freedom.

- Samson lost his purpose.

So many of us start with so much and end up with so little. Samson became a judge—a political icon but he found himself on a path of self-destruction and fell from glory to shame. Samson had the authority to dictate to others and now, others were dictating to him. He once had dominion and found himself being dominated. Samson lost all control of his life. He was in the custody of the enemy.

When the enemy takes away your authority over your own life, that means he can control you. He can rearrange your plans. He can call the shots. He can set his own agenda for your life. Never put yourself in a position where you no longer have the ability to manage your life. Clearly, we see that obedience to the Will of God keeps you on a straight path to your destiny.

Never put yourself in a position where you no longer have the ability to manage your life.

Samson lost his vision. He lost his natural vision as well as his spiritual vision. Loss of vision is a major roadblock to your destiny. The Philistines put out his eyes physically and spiritually. The enemy always wants to cause you to lose your vision. Without a vision for your life, you will perish.

Loss of vision is a major roadblock to your destiny.

Proverbs 29:18 (KJV)

18 Where there is no vision, the people perish

You cannot take back what you cannot see. If the enemy can wipe out your ability to see (perceive), you will be forever lost.

- Without vision, you can't see where you are supposed to be.

- Without vision, you can never grasp the understanding of your pre-natal assignment.

- Without vision, you cannot walk according to God's plan for your life.

So, naturally and spiritually, the enemy will seek to destroy your vision. When your sight is directed toward the things of this world, you are blinded to the things of God.

When your sight is directed toward the things of this world, you are blinded to the things of God.

---

1 John 2 :16

For all that is in the world, the lust of the flesh, and the lust of the eyes, and the pride of life, is not of the Father, but is of the world. 17 And the world passeth away, and the lust thereof: but he that doeth the will of God abideth for ever.

Let me take you back to the beginning. The Bible says that God blessed man and God gave man specific instructions for his destiny.

"Be fruitful, multiply, replenish the earth and subdue it and have dominion."

Be fruitful, multiply, replenish the earth and subdue it and have dominion.

Dominion means to be on top. The plan of the devil is to bring you down. But, God has declared that your destiny is up and not down. Down is not your destiny! The Bible says you are above and not beneath. You are the head and not the tail. It further declares that you are a Royal priesthood, a chosen generation, a peculiar people. When you follow the Lord and lean on Him, He will always guide you in the right direction. His lead will never take you down.

Psalm 119:105

Your word is a lamp unto my feet and a light unto my path.

When you allow the Word of God to chart your course, when you are walking in His Spirit, when you are living a life that is pleasing to God, you will find yourself in His Will. His Will for your life is that you complete your pre-natal assignment and walk in his prescribed destiny for your life.

The Apostle Paul understood the struggle that Samson had, for he also struggled with his flesh. That is why the Apostle implores us, as Christians, to present our bodies a living sacrifice, holy, and acceptable unto God. The Apostle Paul admonishes us not to be conformed to this world but to be transformed by the renewing of our minds.

Romans 12:1-2 (KJV)

1 I beseech you therefore, brethren, by the mercies of God, that ye present your bodies a living sacrifice, holy, acceptable unto God, which is your reasonable service.

2 And be not conformed to this world: but be ye transformed by the renewing of your mind, that ye may prove what is that good, and acceptable, and perfect, will of God.

You have to get your mind right so you can discern God's Will for your life.

- When your mind is right, you can cast down every imagination and everything that exalts itself against the knowledge of God.

- When your mind is right, you have no fellowship with unfruitful works of darkness.

- When your mind is right, you put on the whole armor of God, so that you can stand against the wiles of the devil.

Samson lost his mind to the world and, as a result, he lost his dominion and his status. He lost his authority. He went from up to down. He was consumed by the fire he was sent to put out. The devil is a destiny-blocker. His plan is to turn your life upside down and to destroy your future.

The devil is a destiny-blocker. His plan is to turn your life upside down and to destroy your future.

John 10:10 (KJV)

10 The thief cometh not, but for to steal, and to kill, and to destroy: I am come that they might have life, and that they might have it more abundantly.

Samson lost his freedom. The Bible says, "and bound him with fetters of bronze." That is the devil at his best. He uses you up and then he leaves you bound.

- drug addiction

- alcoholism

- sexual perversion

- gambling

- fornication

- lying

- stealing

The devil's plan is to keep you in bondage to all of the above. He wants to keep you in bondage so that you can never carry out the pre-natal assignment on your life. His plan is to enslave you and cause you to be dysfunctional. When you are in bondage, you cannot move freely in the plan of God for your life.

_____

When you are in bondage, you cannot move freely in the plan of God for your life.

When you are in bondage, you are of no use to God. God's plan for you is that you walk in liberty. His plan for you is that you have life and have it more abundantly. Conversely, Hell's plan is for you to lose your purpose. Samson lost his purpose.

Judges 16:21 (KJV)

21 But the Philistines took him, and put out his eyes, and brought him down to Gaza, and bound him with fetters of brass; and he did grind in the prison house.

Here is a man who was called to great things. He was to be the leader of Israel. God had pre-destined him to represent Israel on His behalf. He was a man born with a great purpose. He was a Nazarite set apart unto God in his mother's womb. He had a great pre-natal assignment on his life, but he embraced a life of sin which was a major roadblock to his destiny.

Judges 13:5 (KJV)

5 For, lo, thou shalt conceive, and bear a son; and no razor shall come on his head: for the child shall be a Nazarite unto God from the womb: and he shall begin to deliver Israel out of the hand of the Philistines.

As you go through the pages of this book, there is something that you should keep in your hearts and let it become a mantra for your daily lives—"Outside of the presence of God, there is nothing."

- You cannot reach your destiny without God.

- You cannot fulfill your purpose without God.

- You cannot carry out your pre-natal assignment without God.

"Outside of the presence of God, there is nothing."

God is neither an alternative nor an option. He is not Eeny, Meeny Miny, or Moe in the game of life. We need God. Just like the plants need soil—we need God. Just like the fish need water—we need God. We cannot fulfill our purpose or bear any fruit apart from God. God made everyone with a distinct purpose.

We cannot fulfill our purpose or bear any fruit apart from God.

Whenever you have roadblocks, you have to make detours in order to reach your destination. Samson experienced a major roadblock to his destiny by embracing a life of compromise and sin. As a result, he no longer experienced the presence of God.

Sometimes, in life, you will face roadblocks but, if your desire is to get to your prescribed destination, you will seek out the detours. You have to overcome the obstacles and find a path that will take you where God wants you to go. It is never too late for a U-Turn to get back in the presence of God.

It is never too late for a U-Turn to get back in the presence of God.

Samson cried out to God in prayer and prayer put him back in the presence of God. Prayer was his way back to his destiny and his way back to God. Samson cried out to God and because of his faith God revisited Samson and he regained his strength. The Bible says that the dead that he slew at his death were more than they whom he slew in his life.

Judges 16:28-30 (KJV)

28 And Samson called unto the LORD, and said, O Lord GOD, remember me, I pray thee, and strengthen me, I pray thee, only this once, O God, that I may be at once avenged of the Philistines for my two eyes.

29 And Samson took hold of the two middle pillars upon which the house stood, and on which it was borne up, of the one with his right hand, and of the other with his left.

*30 And Samson said, Let me die with the
Philistines. And he bowed himself with all his
might; and the house fell upon the lords, and upon
all the people that were therein.
So the dead which he slew at his death were more
than they which he slew in his life.*

Samson got back into the presence of God through a prayer of faith. When you are out from under God's Will and the presence of the Lord is not with you, a simple prayer of repentance can put you back in His presence.

Be encouraged today. You might have been faced with some major roadblocks to your destiny and you are trying to figure out how to get back on course. You can recover quickly and advance in a new direction. You can make that U-Turn and come back to God. God is a prayer-answering God. Just like He answered Samson's prayer, He will answer yours. God answers prayers.

Lord, remember me!!!

Chapter Seven

THE MIDWAY PASSAGE

Any assignment from God carries with it the weight of its own experience. Each person has to endure his own trials and challenges. Everyone's assignment is different and each assignment comes with its own set of instructions. There is a predetermined season that has been sovereignly chosen by God for you to carry out your pre-natal assignment. This season is consistent with and conducive to the Will of God for your life. God, in His sovereignty, on His calendar in eternity, blocked off a specific season for your pre-natal assignment to be completed on earth.

God in His sovereignty, on His calendar in eternity, blocked off a specific season for your pre-natal assignment to be completed on earth.

It is a time when time intersects with purpose—"Kairos time." It is the right and opportune moment; not a moment too soon or too late. It is not governed by a chronometer. It is not about "Tick Tock." This is a season of proper alignment between the divine and the natural. It is divinely synchronized to accommodate the pre-natal assignment for your life. Those who are lazy and those who lack discernment will miss their "kairos moment."

"Kairos time" is a pre-requisite for purpose to be manifested in the earth realm. It is supreme time. It is as though God, Himself, takes His finger and systematically directs the course of events. Everything has been set in place for you to carry out the assignment.

Each assignment has a starting date and a finishing date and a whole lot of time in the middle, where doubts and fears rise up to test your character and your conviction of purpose. It is in the middle that many of us falter and give up. The middle is where you feel like turning back. The middle is a true test for those who seek to run the race that leads to their prophetic destiny. How many of us have had to go with God even when we did not know where He was taking us?

The middle is a true test for those who seek to run the race that leads to their prophetic destiny.

Genesis 12:1 (KJV)

1 Now the LORD had said unto Abram, Get thee out of thy country, and from thy kindred, and from thy father's house, unto a land that I will shew thee:

Many dreams and visions are lost in the middle of the journey. Your faith and determination is tested in the "midway passage." You begin the journey with great determination to go all the way and you look forward with great anticipation to the end but the middle is where you get impatient and your faith begins to wane.

However, as long as you are still in the race, you can make it to the finish line. Those who choose to forfeit the race end up as life-losers and never know what it is like to experience the throes of victory. The interesting thing about running the race and going all the way to the finish line is that you compete against no one but yourself.

Each person has his own assignment and must deal with the plagues of his own heart. All of us have to govern our own fears and doubts as we navigate our way through the obstacles that confront us in the middle of the journey. The "midway passage" tests and challenges your own faith. It is your own commitment to succeed that is tried and tested.

There might be many participants in the race, but we are individually judged by our own efforts and our own determination to maximize our potential. How we face the challenges of the "midway passage" determines whether or not we complete our pre-natal assignment. Opportunity comes with two invitations. It invites you to succeed or fail and it is incumbent on all of us to make the correct choice.

How we face the challenges of the "midway passage" determines whether or not we complete our pre-natal assignment.

Every choice that we make in life builds a character profile and each choice either takes us toward or away from fulfilling God's plan for our lives. We don't always know where the assignment might take us, but we know, beyond doubt, that God is with us wherever we go.

Joshua 24:15 (KJV)

15 And if it seem evil unto you to serve the LORD, choose you this day whom ye will serve; whether the gods which your fathers served that were on the other side of the flood, or the gods of the Amorites, in whose land ye dwell: but as for me

> *and my house, we will serve the LORD.*

The route to your destiny can be treacherous and exacting. It requires dogged determination and persistence to maneuver the obstacle course of life. It requires strong faith and a burning desire to please God through obedience to his instructions. Many of us find ourselves in the Valley of Baca. Dreams and visions are buried in that valley.

The Valley of Baca was part of the desert country that the pilgrims would have to go through on their way to worship in Jerusalem. The valley was infiltrated with life-threatening agents. It was covered with thorns, vicious animals, pitfalls, vipers, and all sorts of danger. There were wells in Baca, but they were far apart and generally inaccessible. Anyone who traveled this valley would face the threat of death and extreme suffering. This valley was also known as "the valley of tears."

There are times in our lives, in our quest to carry out our pre-natal assignment that we have to go through "Baca." The "midway passage" is likened unto "Baca." It is in this valley that the mantle of obedience is tried and tested. The perils of the "midway passage" require a means beyond us to be victorious—we need God!

The perils of the "midway passage" require a means beyond us to be victorious—we need God!

Many find themselves shackled and fettered from the strongholds that seek to deter them from completing their assignment. The corpses of many would-be Pastors, Evangelists, Prophets, Teachers and Apostles are buried in this valley. They lay in the company of other "would-bees:" psalmists, doctors, teachers, scientists, and so many others. These are they who started out with a mind to complete the pre-natal assignment for their lives, but could not endure the demands of the "midway passage."

God has given us some tools to help us endure the "midway passage." There are some wells from which we can draw. These wells enable us to experience times of refreshing and renewal to make it to the finish line. We are able to go beyond our own strength and focus on the thirst-quenching wells and not on the dryness of the land.

Praise is a well from which we can draw, to re-ignite the fire and the determination to continue. Praise floods the heart with assuredness that in spite of what it looks like, we serve a God who is bigger than our circumstances and a God who is bigger than our valleys. Even David, the great warrior of many battles, discovered the value of praise in the valley.

Praise is a well from which we can draw and re-ignite the fire and the determination to continue.

Psalm 84:5-7 (KJV)

5 Blessed is the man whose strength is in thee; in whose heart are the ways of them.

6 Who passing through the valley of Baca make it a well; the rain also filleth the pools.

7 They go from strength to strength, every one of them in Zion appeareth before God.

The Valley of Baca is laden with corpses of potential that stand to remind us that, unless we allow God to be our guide, we can die in the valley and never get to complete our assignment.

If you find yourself in the "midway passage" and you are contemplating whether to quit or to continue, I recommend that even where you are, begin to draw from the well of praise. You might be overwhelmed and weary, but dig deep down and find a praise in your belly that will confuse the enemy.

The "midway passage" can be your valley of praise where you survive the satanic attacks that come to counter what God has called you to do. Stop what you are doing right now and begin to praise God. Give him the highest praise. Halellujah!!!

The "midway passage" can be your valley of praise where you survive the satanic attacks that come to counter what God has called you to do.

Do not settle for failure. God has given you the necessary measure for you to be victorious. The middle is only an indication that you are half way out. Challenge yourself to keep going. "Baca" is not your station. It is only a path that you must traverse to get where God wants you to be. God has given you the authority to annihilate every counter-attack from the enemy. With faith in Christ, you can quench every fiery dart of the enemy. You have the power to tread upon serpents and scorpions. Take authority over the valley and begin to praise your way out.

Luke 10:19 (KJV)

19 Behold, I give unto you power to tread on serpents and scorpions, and over all the power of the enemy: and nothing shall by any means hurt you.

"Midway praisers" are the testimony bearers. They are the ones who live to tell about the goodness of the Lord in the land of the living. They are the ones who have witnessed God supernaturally move on their behalf. They have witnessed the walls come tumbling down after a midway praise. They have stood under the cloud by day and slept under the pillar of fire by night. "Midway praisers" know what it is like to praise God in the night season. They have wept at night but they are able to embrace the new morning as they witness God turn their mourning into joy.

"Midway praisers" are the testimony bearers.

The Bible says that God inhabits the praises of His people. So, you might be going through the worst trial of your life, but praise Him anyhow. You might be going through the valley of the shadow of death, but praise Him anyhow.

Psalm 23:4 (KJV)

4 Yea, though I walk through the valley of the shadow of death, I will fear no evil: for thou art with me; thy rod and thy staff they comfort me.

When you give God a "valley praise," it is a clear indication that you trust God. A "valley praise" sends a clear message to the devil that you are not moved by your circumstance but you are moved by God. You are declaring that the God of the mountain is the same God of the valley. He is with you if you are up and He is with you if you are down.

Your praise in the valley elevates you to the mountain top and unlocks the door to your destiny. The devil's plan is to keep you trapped in the valley so you cannot get to the mountain top. But when you praise God in the valley experience, it totally confuses the enemy and it breaks the shackles of bondage.

Today, far too many of us in the church do not understand the power of praise. Somehow, praise has been defined as something we do when God pleases us. Praising God, only when we are on the receiving end of tangible blessings, reveals that our love for God is conditional and we have reduced God to a cosmic Santa Claus. True praise is demonstrated when you can't see the end anywhere in sight.

True praise is demonstrated when you can't see the end anywhere in sight.

Praise should never be determined by your circumstances. You do not praise God when things are going well and stop when challenges arise. You praise Him continuously in the good and the bad; in the beginning, the end, and also in the middle. It is to be a continuous melody of recognition and honor to the great God of the universe—the One who providentially delegates your pre-natal assignment.

Psalm 34:1-2 (KJV)

1 I will bless the LORD at all times: his praise shall continually be in my mouth.

2 My soul shall make her boast in the LORD: the humble shall hear thereof, and be glad.

A true praise emerges out of a state of despair—when you have lost everything—but you still praise God for who He is. You might not understand what in the world is going on, and you might be confused and about ready to lose your mind, but you still praise God.

You might be down in the valley and the end seems to be nowhere in sight, but you must still have a praise in your belly. When you release your praise, it will shoot up to heaven and echo in the valley. It will usher in an anointing that removes every obstacle out of your way. Praise Him! Praise is the mechanism by which God meets us where we are.

Praise is the mechanism by which God meets us where we are.

Chapter Eight

THE EULOGY

In every man's life, there are moments of reflection as we draw close to the end of our journey here on earth. Retrospectively, we review our "things to do list" and we either beg for more time or we are fully satisfied with our accomplishments.

It is quite an apocalypse to realize that you are at the end of your life's journey and you are still full of those things that should have been deposited in the earth. The book was never written; the song was never sung; the story was never told; the mountain was never scaled. Your gift was never exposed to the world.

There comes a time when you have to answer hard questions. How many have heard the good news about Jesus Christ from your lips? How did you handle the roadblocks on your journey? Did you survive the "midway passage"? How many lives have been touched or changed because you completed your pre-natal assignment?

2 Timothy 4:6-8 (KJV)

6 For I am now ready to be offered, and the time of my departure is at hand.

7 I have fought a good fight, I have finished my course, I have kept the faith:

8 Henceforth there is laid up for me a crown of righteousness, which the Lord, the righteous judge, shall give me at that day: and not to me only, but unto all them also that love his appearing

The Apostle, Paul, as he spoke to young Timothy found himself in a moment of reflection. He looked back over the history of his life and how he handled his pre-natal assignment.

With great assuredness, he looks ahead during his final lap and, with the finish line before him, declares to Timothy his self-assessment of how he completed his pre-natal assignment. I imagine that Paul might have had tears of joy in his eyes as he gave a summary of the race he ran and the great hope of his future beyond his death.

It is inevitable that there will be a day when each of us will come to the end of our own race. It will no longer be about the precipitous journey of our past nor the humbling state of our departure. It will be about a future, beyond this earth, in eternity, where we were first conceived in the mind of God.

The goal of every man should be to hear, "well done," and wear his crown of jewels in eternity with Jesus Christ. He is the One who died for us and because He died, we can live forever.

Most going home services are decorated with nice little programs expressing the sunrise and the sunset. Families and friends and perhaps a prestigious person will say flowery things about you.

The program will include a spot for "the eulogy" where one person will pretend to be the final judge and declare everything good about you and then you are laid to rest. While family members and friends are showering you with compliments and saluting you for all the good you have done, your works have already been judged as it relates to your pre-natal assignment.

Salvation is not earned by your works. It is a free gift of God. It is by grace, alone, that man is saved through faith in Jesus Christ. However, you are still accountable for the pre-natal assignment for your life.

Beyond capricious outbursts of Hallelujahs and sounds of mourning, there is another eulogy that you should "live" to receive. This eulogy far exceeds any compliments, praise, or accolades that man could bestow upon you. It is recognition from our Creator. He gives us the final grade for our pre-natal assignment. It should be the desire of every person that they receive a great "welcome home" and not a dismissal from God.

Matthew 25:23 (KJV)

23 Well done, good and faithful servant . . . ;

Matthew 7:22-23 (KJV)

22 Many will say to me in that day, Lord, Lord, have we not prophesied in thy name? and in thy name have cast out devils? and in thy name done many wonderful works?

23 And then will I profess unto them, I never knew you: depart from me, ye that work iniquity.

It is required of all of us to answer the Clarion Call of God and to complete the pre-natal assignment for our lives. There is a course that is laid out for us that is consistent with the assignment from God. This course must be followed in order to hear, "well done!" The course is laid out in the Bible and cannot be circumvented nor can it be avoided. There is no room for mediocrity and self-destructive choices. The success of our Christian life is not measured by how fast we sprint out of the starting block. Victory comes by staying the course and crossing the finish line. How we handle our pre-natal assignment will determine whether we die empty or full.

Chapter Nine

MY TESTIMONY

I give all praise and honor to my Lord and Savior, Jesus Christ. I give thanks to the Holy Spirit for His enabling power.

In writing this book, I was forced to come to grips with my own pre-natal assignment. I realize that there are many sub-assignments that are a part of the pre-natal assignment. I thank God for opening up my eyes when he did. For years, I stumbled around in darkness. I was like the ship on the ocean without a compass. When I reflect and I remember some of the choices I made in my own life and live to tell about them, I know that God is a loving God.

My priority had nothing to do with God. Life in the fast lane was the thrust of my life. You name it, I did it. What was seemingly fun was always challenged by my desire to discover self. I was having fun, but there was an emptiness that lived on the inside of me and little did I know that the emptiness could only be filled if I allowed God to be in control of my life. I thought I had all the answers. I totally depended upon self-government and God was not on my radar.

I knew about God. I knew that He was the Creator of heaven and earth and He was the Giver of all life. I knew about the virgin birth and that Jesus was the Savior of the world. I was familiar with prayer and on many occasions, I engaged God in a conversation about my needs. I read the Bible and was particularly comforted with the Psalms. From time to time, I would go to church and I would leave just as empty as I entered.

However, as much as I thought I knew about God and as much as I would periodically engage Him in long talks about me, I never knew Him. I did not have an intimate relationship with Him.

It was July 29, 1989 that I came to a place in my life where I realized that I needed God. That was the night I accepted Jesus Christ as my personal Savior and made a commitment to serve Him for the rest of my life. Something inexplicable happened when I gave my life to Christ. It was as though God had literally taken His fingers and opened my eyes.

At the time I gave my life to Christ, I had no idea of anything called a pre-natal assignment. I just knew that I needed God. There was such a great emptiness on the inside of me and nothing that I tried was able to fill the void. I knew that there was more to my life than what I had lived. Now that I had surrendered my life to Christ, the eyes of my understanding were opened. I could now read the Bible and walk away with understanding of the Word of God. God began to reveal His mysteries to me.

One Saturday morning, in March 1990, I had an encounter with God that is forever etched in my memory. I was driving on the highway and God gave me a special visitation. It was as though God hijacked my car and I ended up in a remote parking lot miles away from my house. The Shekinah Glory of God fell in the car. I was caught up in a zone that was foreign to me. In a vision, I saw a globe that came out of heaven. There was a ribbon wrapped around the globe and on the ribbon was written, "my brother's keeper." The globe jetted across the sky and, finally, it landed on a building and the ribbon left the globe and was stretched out above the door of the building.

I will never forget the echoing voice that spoke with so much authority as God commanded me to preach His gospel—"Go preach my gospel." My response was just like Jeremiah's. God and I pretty much had the same conversation and I was no match for God. I cried so hard as I fearfully surrendered and answered, "Yes," to the call of God.

I was weakened by the power of God and after about one hour of just bawling, I humbly made my way home at about 10 miles per hour. When I got home, I got on my knees in front of my bed and the Spirit of God put me to sleep. I slept for about 4 hours on my knees.

When I awoke, it was as though I was in a new land. Everything looked fresh and new. To my surprise, while I was asleep, God had downloaded sermons in me and new words were introduced to my vocabulary.

From that day, I have given myself to God and I have allowed God to raise me up according to His plan for my life. I trusted God with my life and still do. Now, as I look back over my Christian walk, I am amazed at how God has directed the course of my life.

I am married to a wonderful man of God, Pastor Benjamin W. Rucker. I serve as the Assistant Pastor of Bride of Christ Church Ministries, Int'l. We oversee churches all over the world. So many lives have been changed as God uses us to minister, globally.

Each day, I renew my commitment to be used by God for His purpose. God has directed my path across several continents to minister healing and restoration to the lost. He has taken me beyond geographical boundaries to preach and teach the gospel of Jesus Christ. Many have come to know the saving knowledge of the Lord, Jesus Christ.

Cradle of H.O.P.E. is a Foundation that God directed me to start. Needy children all over the world benefit from this Foundation.

I have given my life away to Jesus and I trust Him to continue to lead me as I press forward to complete my pre-natal assignment—a prophet to the nations.

To God be the glory!

About The Author

ANGELA MARIE RUCKER, Th.D., D.D.

Dr. Angela Rucker is an international minister, lecturer, and visionary leader.

Travelling extensively throughout the world, Dr. Rucker ministers restoration to people who are broken and void of purpose. Dr. Rucker delves into the issues of life and presents an alternative to all of life's struggles. The focus of her ministry is to teach people how to "Walk in Dominion" so they can discover self and move from brokenness to wholeness.

Dr. Rucker serves as the Assistant Pastor of Bride of Christ Church Ministries, International located in Mitchellville, MD., USA. She is the President and Chief Executive Officer of Cradle of H.O.P.E., Inc. Foundation.

Dr. Rucker earned a Doctorate in Theology from Andersonville Theological Seminary. She was also awarded an Honorary Doctorate in Divinity from Eastern North Carolina Theological Institute.

Dr. Rucker and her husband, Benjamin, serve together as a team. They are called to go beyond geographical boundaries to teach and preach the uncompromising Word of God. They travel together and plant many churches, globally.